A NEW MIND

SET IN SOUL

© 2020 Tatiana Media LLC in partnership with Set In Soul LLC

ISBN #:978-1-949874-82-2

Published by Tatiana Media LLC

For general information on our other products and services, please contact our Customer Support within the United States at support@setinsoul.com.

Tatiana Media LLC as well as Set In Soul LLC publishes its books in a variety of electronic formats. Some content that appears in print may not be available in electronic books.

THIS JOURNAL BELONGS TO

_____

DEDICATED TO FEELING GOOD.
DEDICATED TO BEING FREE.

March 4th 2022

So I bought this workbook awhile ago but didn't really have the nerve or the strength to open it up and deal with it; but now I have to because things have gone from bad to worse. I'm in a bad place and I want to get out of it. Once again I'm unhappy in a marriage. That seems to be harder work than it needs to be. I'm somewhat to blame but not 100%. Alcohol is and will be the biggest problem... and I know it; girls, boys. The dogs hate when we fight and we only really fight when we drink. I don't like it but I continue to do it. I guess sometimes I feel like I won't lose the people or things that I seemingly treasure the most. I don't like being called a dumbass bitch. No one who cares as deeply as I do should ever be called that. This marriage is very difficult. I don't know how happy I am with any of it but what choice do I have?

TABLE OF CONTENTS

HOW TO USE THIS JOURNAL

Negative thinking is mainly apprehension or fear-based. Simply put, negative thinking is the fear of the indefinite, the effects of your past on your today, fear of what lies ahead, unhealed anger and hurt, a distorted self-image and/or even the inability to cope and deal with people and/or situations. All these things and many more can trigger negative thoughts. Negative thinking can mentally, emotionally and physically imprison you when you continue to entertain them. It is the overthinking of negative thoughts that can lead to actions of self-destruction. What must be realized is that you cannot prevent a negative fearful thought from ever happening again but you can dismiss negative thoughts and immediately counter it with a positive thought. It is all on what you choose to focus on and we want you to focus on your greatest good because as you know what you think about is what you become.

Your thoughts inspire your emotions which fuel your actions. So to gain peace of mind as well as regain your ability to focus on your goals and manifest the best life for yourself, a positive mind is needed. A mind that consistently works for you and not against you. Your thoughts can be your best friend making you feel like life is great or it can be your worst enemy making you feel as if things in your life can never get better. With this journal you can start to take control of your thoughts by first getting to the root of the thought, then recognizing the pattern of which they enter your conscience mind and lastly learning how to quickly curate a positive believable thought to counter the negative thought. Now is the best time to recognize and break harmful thought influences.

We recommend filing out this journal every morning and night. This journal requires you to be truthful and gentle with yourself. It is with this journal you can feel free because this is your no judgement zone. You are restructuring and recreating your thoughts with this journal. The motivational quotes sprinkled throughout this journal are there to inspire you to stay on track with your efforts to rebuild a new you with a new mind, so let's get started.

I AM
EXPOSING

I AM EXPOSING

I Have Negative Thoughts Towards:

most of the choices I've made
in my life.

These Things Promote Negative Thoughts Within Me:

I Do Not Believe:

Negative Thoughts I Have Towards Myself:

What Do I Focus On That Is Negative?

I AM EXPOSING

What Past Experience Have I Had That Have Impacted Me Negatively?

What Am I Insecure About?

I Am Secure About:

It Really Hurts Me When:

I Tend To Overthink:

I AM EXPOSING

What Influences My Negative Thoughts?

What Negative Thoughts Have I Held On To That Are Facts?

What Negative Thoughts Have I Held On To That Are Opinions?

Are My Thoughts Allowing Me To Jump To Conclusions?

Thinking The Way I Do Has Caused Me To Feel:

I AM EXPOSING

Thinking The Way I Do Has Caused Me To Act:

The Advantages Of Thinking These Thoughts:

The Disadvantages Of Thinking These Thoughts:

What Do I Take Personally?

What Have I Took Personally?

I AM EXPOSING

When I Do Not Meet My Own Expectations:

When Other People Do Not Meet My Expectations:

Do I Exaggerate?

What Can I Do To Challenge My Negative Thoughts?

What Positive Things Would I Like To Focus On?

I AM EXPOSING

When I Think I Can Not Do 'This' (Whatever This Is), I:

When I Think The Thought 'I Can Not Do This,' I Can Change This Thought To:

When I Think The Thought 'I Am Not Good Enough,' I Can Change This Thought To:

When I Think The Thought 'What If It Does Not Work Out?,' I Can Change This Thought To:

When I Think The Thought 'I Do Not Like The Way I Look,' I Can Change This Thought To:

I AM EXPOSING

I Am Proud Of:

Is There A Reason To Hold On To Any Of My Negative Thoughts?

If Yes To The Previous Prompt, What Is The Reason?

My Negative Thoughts Have Caused Me To:

The Root Of These Negative Thoughts Come From:

I AM EXPOSING

What Are My Negative Thoughts Towards Others?

The Root Of My Negative Thoughts Towards Others:

How Do Negative Thoughts Affect Me?

How Much Time Do I Spend Entertaining Negative Thoughts?

It Is Much Easier For Me To Think These Thoughts:

I AM EXPOSING

How Do I View People?

My Philosophy On People:

How Often Do My Negative Thoughts Pop Up Each Day?

I Believe Negative Thoughts Are:

What Feelings Spark Negative Thoughts?

I AM EXPOSING

What Do I Do That Continues To Fuel Negative Thoughts?

What Am I Afraid Of?

How Can I Beat My Fears?

Are My Negative Thoughts Founded On Fear?

Why Do My Fears Speak Louder Than My Strengths And Beliefs
(Answer If Applicable)?

I AM EXPOSING

Moving Forward:

I Understand That:

I Will No Longer Allow Any Negative Thought:

How Can I Be There For Me?

How Can I Protect Myself From Entertaining Any New Negative Thoughts?

I AM EXPOSING

I Believe Thinking Positive Will Help Me:

By Thinking Positive, I Know I Will Gain:

Anytime A Negative Thought Arises I Will:

I Will Deliberately:

I Rather Think About:

I AM EXPOSING

What Makes Me Feel Good?

I Want To Live My Life:

I Will Make Feeling Good Louder Than:

How Often Do I Mediate?

I Embrace:

I AM EXPOSING

I Like To Guide My Thoughts:

I Am Good At Identifying:

It Is Easy For Me To Feel Good About:

What Do I Want?

I Need To Forgive:

I AM EXPOSING

What Happened In The Past That Has Caused Me To Form Negative Thoughts?

Why Does What Happened In The Previous Prompt Still Matter?

What Does The Answer In The Previous Prompt Change?

What Happened In The Past Currently Affects Me By:

When Something Goes Wrong, How Do I 'Let It Go?'

I AM EXPOSING

I Feel That I Lack:

I Do Not Have To Figure Out Right Now:

When Something Unwanted Happens, I Tend To Think:

How Will I Start Creating New Positive Thoughts When Something Unwanted Happens To Me?

It Is Easy For Me To Think:

I AM EXPOSING

Negative Scenerios I Have Made Up In My Mind:

I Am Aware Of:

Deliberate Thoughts I Have Created:

A
NEW
BELIEF

A NEW BELIEF
MORNING THOUGHTS

Date: My Mood:

Today's Affirmation: Today I Am Releasing:

Today's New Beliefs: Today I Am Choosing To Feel:

NIGHTLY THOUGHTS

Today I Chose To See: Today I Noticed A Positive Change In:

Today I Forgave: I Stopped Criticizing Myself And
                                     Started Saying:

Today I Expected: A Naturally Good Feeling Thought:

When I Got Or Did Not Get What I   When I Conversed With Someone
Expected, I: Who Was Feeling Bad About
                                     Themselves Or Complaining, I:

Today I Stretched My Beliefs By: A List Of Some Positive Thoughts I
                                     Had Today That I Did Not Oppose
                                     With Negative Thoughts:

A NEW BELIEF
MORNING THOUGHTS

Date: My Mood:

Today's Affirmation: Today I Am Releasing:

Today's New Beliefs: Today I Am Choosing To Feel:

NIGHTLY THOUGHTS

Today I Chose To See: Today I Noticed A Positive Change In:

Today I Forgave: I Stopped Criticizing Myself And
                                   Started Saying:

Today I Expected: A Naturally Good Feeling Thought:

When I Got Or Did Not Get What I   When I Conversed With Someone
Expected, I: Who Was Feeling Bad About
                                   Themselves Or Complaining, I:

Today I Stretched My Beliefs By: A List Of Some Positive Thoughts I
                                   Had Today That I Did Not Oppose
                                   With Negative Thoughts:

A NEW BELIEF
<u>MORNING THOUGHTS</u>

Date: My Mood:

Today's Affirmation: Today I Am Releasing:

Today's New Beliefs: Today I Am Choosing To Feel:

<u>NIGHTLY THOUGHTS</u>

Today I Chose To See: Today I Noticed A Positive Change In:

Today I Forgave: I Stopped Criticizing Myself And
                                         Started Saying:

Today I Expected: A Naturally Good Feeling Thought:

When I Got Or Did Not Get What I   When I Conversed With Someone
Expected, I: Who Was Feeling Bad About
                                         Themselves Or Complaining, I:

Today I Stretched My Beliefs By: A List Of Some Positive Thoughts I
                                         Had Today That I Did Not Oppose
                                         With Negative Thoughts:

I WILL NOT ALLOW NEGATIVE THOUGHTS TO DICTATE MY ATTITUDE.

A NEW BELIEF
MORNING THOUGHTS

Date: My Mood:

Today's Affirmation: Today I Am Releasing:

Today's New Beliefs: Today I Am Choosing To Feel:

NIGHTLY THOUGHTS

Today I Chose To See: Today I Noticed A Positive Change In:

Today I Forgave: I Stopped Criticizing Myself And
                                         Started Saying:

Today I Expected: A Naturally Good Feeling Thought:

When I Got Or Did Not Get What I   When I Conversed With Someone
Expected, I: Who Was Feeling Bad About
                                         Themselves Or Complaining, I:

Today I Stretched My Beliefs By: A List Of Some Positive Thoughts I
                                         Had Today That I Did Not Oppose
                                         With Negative Thoughts:

A NEW BELIEF
MORNING THOUGHTS

Date: My Mood:

Today's Affirmation: Today I Am Releasing:

Today's New Beliefs: Today I Am Choosing To Feel:

NIGHTLY THOUGHTS

Today I Chose To See: Today I Noticed A Positive Change In:

Today I Forgave: I Stopped Criticizing Myself And
                                         Started Saying:

Today I Expected: A Naturally Good Feeling Thought:

When I Got Or Did Not Get What I   When I Conversed With Someone
Expected, I: Who Was Feeling Bad About
                                         Themselves Or Complaining, I:

Today I Stretched My Beliefs By: A List Of Some Positive Thoughts I
                                         Had Today That I Did Not Oppose
                                         With Negative Thoughts:

NEGATIVE THOUGHTS COME FROM OVERTHINKING.

MY THOUGHTS ARE TOO POWERFUL TO SPEND TIME THINKING ABOUT ANYTHING THAT DOES NOT MAKE ME HAPPY.

A NEW BELIEF
MORNING THOUGHTS

Date: My Mood:

Today's Affirmation: Today I Am Releasing:

Today's New Beliefs: Today I Am Choosing To Feel:

NIGHTLY THOUGHTS

Today I Chose To See: Today I Noticed A Positive Change In:

Today I Forgave: I Stopped Criticizing Myself And
                                Started Saying:

Today I Expected: A Naturally Good Feeling Thought:

When I Got Or Did Not Get What I   When I Conversed With Someone
Expected, I: Who Was Feeling Bad About
                                    Themselves Or Complaining, I:

Today I Stretched My Beliefs By: A List Of Some Positive Thoughts I
                                    Had Today That I Did Not Oppose
                                    With Negative Thoughts:

A NEW BELIEF
MORNING THOUGHTS

Date: My Mood:

Today's Affirmation: Today I Am Releasing:

Today's New Beliefs: Today I Am Choosing To Feel:

NIGHTLY THOUGHTS

Today I Chose To See: Today I Noticed A Positive Change In:

Today I Forgave: I Stopped Criticizing Myself And
                                   Started Saying:

Today I Expected: A Naturally Good Feeling Thought:

When I Got Or Did Not Get What I   When I Conversed With Someone
Expected, I: Who Was Feeling Bad About
                                   Themselves Or Complaining, I:

Today I Stretched My Beliefs By: A List Of Some Positive Thoughts I
                                   Had Today That I Did Not Oppose
                                   With Negative Thoughts:

A NEW BELIEF
MORNING THOUGHTS

Date: My Mood:

Today's Affirmation: Today I Am Releasing:

Today's New Beliefs: Today I Am Choosing To Feel:

NIGHTLY THOUGHTS

Today I Chose To See: Today I Noticed A Positive Change In:

Today I Forgave: I Stopped Criticizing Myself And
                                     Started Saying:

Today I Expected: A Naturally Good Feeling Thought:

When I Got Or Did Not Get What I   When I Conversed With Someone
Expected, I: Who Was Feeling Bad About
                                     Themselves Or Complaining, I:

Today I Stretched My Beliefs By: A List Of Some Positive Thoughts I
                                     Had Today That I Did Not Oppose
                                     With Negative Thoughts:

I CHOOSE TO FOCUS ON THE GOOD.

MY POSITIVE THOUGHTS

A NEW BELIEF
MORNING THOUGHTS

Date: My Mood:

Today's Affirmation: Today I Am Releasing:

Today's New Beliefs: Today I Am Choosing To Feel:

NIGHTLY THOUGHTS

Today I Chose To See: Today I Noticed A Positive Change In:

Today I Forgave: I Stopped Criticizing Myself And
                                         Started Saying:

Today I Expected: A Naturally Good Feeling Thought:

When I Got Or Did Not Get What I   When I Conversed With Someone
Expected, I: Who Was Feeling Bad About
                                         Themselves Or Complaining, I:

Today I Stretched My Beliefs By: A List Of Some Positive Thoughts I
                                         Had Today That I Did Not Oppose
                                         With Negative Thoughts:

A NEW BELIEF
MORNING THOUGHTS

Date: My Mood:

Today's Affirmation: Today I Am Releasing:

Today's New Beliefs: Today I Am Choosing To Feel:

NIGHTLY THOUGHTS

Today I Chose To See: Today I Noticed A Positive Change In:

Today I Forgave: I Stopped Criticizing Myself And
                                         Started Saying:

Today I Expected: A Naturally Good Feeling Thought:

When I Got Or Did Not Get What I   When I Conversed With Someone
Expected, I: Who Was Feeling Bad About
                                         Themselves Or Complaining, I:

Today I Stretched My Beliefs By: A List Of Some Positive Thoughts I
                                         Had Today That I Did Not Oppose
                                         With Negative Thoughts:

A NEW BELIEF
MORNING THOUGHTS

Date: My Mood:

Today's Affirmation: Today I Am Releasing:

Today's New Beliefs: Today I Am Choosing To Feel:

NIGHTLY THOUGHTS

Today I Chose To See: Today I Noticed A Positive Change In:

Today I Forgave: I Stopped Criticizing Myself And
                                     Started Saying:

Today I Expected: A Naturally Good Feeling Thought:

When I Got Or Did Not Get What I   When I Conversed With Someone
Expected, I: Who Was Feeling Bad About
                                     Themselves Or Complaining, I:

Today I Stretched My Beliefs By: A List Of Some Positive Thoughts I
                                     Had Today That I Did Not Oppose
                                     With Negative Thoughts:

MY POSITIVE THOUGHTS

I AM REPLACING NEGATIVE THOUGHTS WITH POSITIVE ONES.

A NEW BELIEF
MORNING THOUGHTS

Date: My Mood:

Today's Affirmation: Today I Am Releasing:

Today's New Beliefs: Today I Am Choosing To Feel:

NIGHTLY THOUGHTS

Today I Chose To See: Today I Noticed A Positive Change In:

Today I Forgave: I Stopped Criticizing Myself And
                               Started Saying:

Today I Expected: A Naturally Good Feeling Thought:

When I Got Or Did Not Get What I   When I Conversed With Someone
Expected, I: Who Was Feeling Bad About
                                    Themselves Or Complaining, I:

Today I Stretched My Beliefs By: A List Of Some Positive Thoughts I
                                    Had Today That I Did Not Oppose
                                    With Negative Thoughts:

A NEW BELIEF
MORNING THOUGHTS

Date: My Mood:

Today's Affirmation: Today I Am Releasing:

Today's New Beliefs: Today I Am Choosing To Feel:

NIGHTLY THOUGHTS

Today I Chose To See: Today I Noticed A Positive Change In:

Today I Forgave: I Stopped Criticizing Myself And
                                         Started Saying:

Today I Expected: A Naturally Good Feeling Thought:

When I Got Or Did Not Get What I   When I Conversed With Someone
Expected, I: Who Was Feeling Bad About
                                         Themselves Or Complaining, I:

Today I Stretched My Beliefs By: A List Of Some Positive Thoughts I
                                         Had Today That I Did Not Oppose
                                         With Negative Thoughts:

MY POSITIVE THOUGHTS

A NEW BELIEF
MORNING THOUGHTS

Date: My Mood:

Today's Affirmation: Today I Am Releasing:

Today's New Beliefs: Today I Am Choosing To Feel:

NIGHTLY THOUGHTS

Today I Chose To See: Today I Noticed A Positive Change In:

Today I Forgave: I Stopped Criticizing Myself And
                                         Started Saying:

Today I Expected: A Naturally Good Feeling Thought:

When I Got Or Did Not Get What I   When I Conversed With Someone
Expected, I: Who Was Feeling Bad About
                                         Themselves Or Complaining, I:

Today I Stretched My Beliefs By: A List Of Some Positive Thoughts I
                                         Had Today That I Did Not Oppose
                                         With Negative Thoughts:

A NEW BELIEF
MORNING THOUGHTS

Date: My Mood:

Today's Affirmation: Today I Am Releasing:

Today's New Beliefs: Today I Am Choosing To Feel:

NIGHTLY THOUGHTS

Today I Chose To See: Today I Noticed A Positive Change In:

Today I Forgave: I Stopped Criticizing Myself And Started Saying:

Today I Expected: A Naturally Good Feeling Thought:

When I Got Or Did Not Get What I Expected, I: When I Conversed With Someone Who Was Feeling Bad About Themselves Or Complaining, I:

Today I Stretched My Beliefs By: A List Of Some Positive Thoughts I Had Today That I Did Not Oppose With Negative Thoughts:

OVERTHINKING MAKES ME FEEL LIKE I DID A WORKOUT AND NOW I NEED TO REST.

A NEW BELIEF
MORNING THOUGHTS

Date: My Mood:

Today's Affirmation: Today I Am Releasing:

Today's New Beliefs: Today I Am Choosing To Feel:

NIGHTLY THOUGHTS

Today I Chose To See: Today I Noticed A Positive Change In:

Today I Forgave: I Stopped Criticizing Myself And
                                         Started Saying:

Today I Expected: A Naturally Good Feeling Thought:

When I Got Or Did Not Get What I   When I Conversed With Someone
Expected, I: Who Was Feeling Bad About
                                         Themselves Or Complaining, I:

Today I Stretched My Beliefs By: A List Of Some Positive Thoughts I
                                         Had Today That I Did Not Oppose
                                         With Negative Thoughts:

A NEW BELIEF
MORNING THOUGHTS

Date: My Mood:

Today's Affirmation: Today I Am Releasing:

Today's New Beliefs: Today I Am Choosing To Feel:

NIGHTLY THOUGHTS

Today I Chose To See: Today I Noticed A Positive Change In:

Today I Forgave: I Stopped Criticizing Myself And
                                         Started Saying:

Today I Expected: A Naturally Good Feeling Thought:

When I Got Or Did Not Get What I   When I Conversed With Someone
Expected, I: Who Was Feeling Bad About
                                         Themselves Or Complaining, I:

Today I Stretched My Beliefs By: A List Of Some Positive Thoughts I
                                         Had Today That I Did Not Oppose
                                         With Negative Thoughts:

A NEW BELIEF
<u>MORNING THOUGHTS</u>

Date: My Mood:

Today's Affirmation: Today I Am Releasing:

Today's New Beliefs: Today I Am Choosing To Feel:

<u>NIGHTLY THOUGHTS</u>

Today I Chose To See: Today I Noticed A Positive Change In:

Today I Forgave: I Stopped Criticizing Myself And
                                         Started Saying:

Today I Expected: A Naturally Good Feeling Thought:

When I Got Or Did Not Get What I   When I Conversed With Someone
Expected, I: Who Was Feeling Bad About
                                         Themselves Or Complaining, I:

Today I Stretched My Beliefs By: A List Of Some Positive Thoughts I
                                         Had Today That I Did Not Oppose
                                         With Negative Thoughts:

A NEW BELIEF
MORNING THOUGHTS

Date: My Mood:

Today's Affirmation: Today I Am Releasing:

Today's New Beliefs: Today I Am Choosing To Feel:

NIGHTLY THOUGHTS

Today I Chose To See: Today I Noticed A Positive Change In:

Today I Forgave: I Stopped Criticizing Myself And
                                   Started Saying:

Today I Expected: A Naturally Good Feeling Thought:

When I Got Or Did Not Get What I   When I Conversed With Someone
Expected, I: Who Was Feeling Bad About
                                   Themselves Or Complaining, I:

Today I Stretched My Beliefs By: A List Of Some Positive Thoughts I
                                   Had Today That I Did Not Oppose
                                   With Negative Thoughts:

MY POSITIVE THOUGHTS

A NEW BELIEF
MORNING THOUGHTS

Date: My Mood:

Today's Affirmation: Today I Am Releasing:

Today's New Beliefs: Today I Am Choosing To Feel:

NIGHTLY THOUGHTS

Today I Chose To See: Today I Noticed A Positive Change In:

Today I Forgave: I Stopped Criticizing Myself And
                                         Started Saying:

Today I Expected: A Naturally Good Feeling Thought:

When I Got Or Did Not Get What I   When I Conversed With Someone
Expected, I: Who Was Feeling Bad About
                                         Themselves Or Complaining, I:

Today I Stretched My Beliefs By: A List Of Some Positive Thoughts I
                                         Had Today That I Did Not Oppose
                                         With Negative Thoughts:

A NEW BELIEF
MORNING THOUGHTS

Date: My Mood:

Today's Affirmation: Today I Am Releasing:

Today's New Beliefs: Today I Am Choosing To Feel:

NIGHTLY THOUGHTS

Today I Chose To See: Today I Noticed A Positive Change In:

Today I Forgave: I Stopped Criticizing Myself And
                                     Started Saying:

Today I Expected: A Naturally Good Feeling Thought:

When I Got Or Did Not Get What I   When I Conversed With Someone
Expected, I: Who Was Feeling Bad About
                                     Themselves Or Complaining, I:

Today I Stretched My Beliefs By: A List Of Some Positive Thoughts I
                                     Had Today That I Did Not Oppose
                                     With Negative Thoughts:

A NEW BELIEF
MORNING THOUGHTS

Date: My Mood:

Today's Affirmation: Today I Am Releasing:

Today's New Beliefs: Today I Am Choosing To Feel:

NIGHTLY THOUGHTS

Today I Chose To See: Today I Noticed A Positive Change In:

Today I Forgave: I Stopped Criticizing Myself And
                                           Started Saying:

Today I Expected: A Naturally Good Feeling Thought:

When I Got Or Did Not Get What I   When I Conversed With Someone
Expected, I: Who Was Feeling Bad About
                                           Themselves Or Complaining, I:

Today I Stretched My Beliefs By: A List Of Some Positive Thoughts I
                                           Had Today That I Did Not Oppose
                                           With Negative Thoughts:

DO NOT BELIEVE EVERY THOUGHT YOU THINK.

WORKING EVERYDAY TO INCREASE THE QUALITY OF MY THOUGHTS.

A NEW BELIEF
MORNING THOUGHTS

Date: My Mood:

Today's Affirmation: Today I Am Releasing:

Today's New Beliefs: Today I Am Choosing To Feel:

NIGHTLY THOUGHTS

Today I Chose To See: Today I Noticed A Positive Change In:

Today I Forgave: I Stopped Criticizing Myself And
                                         Started Saying:

Today I Expected: A Naturally Good Feeling Thought:

When I Got Or Did Not Get What I   When I Conversed With Someone
Expected, I: Who Was Feeling Bad About
                                         Themselves Or Complaining, I:

Today I Stretched My Beliefs By: A List Of Some Positive Thoughts I
                                         Had Today That I Did Not Oppose
                                         With Negative Thoughts:

A NEW BELIEF
MORNING THOUGHTS

Date: My Mood:

Today's Affirmation: Today I Am Releasing:

Today's New Beliefs: Today I Am Choosing To Feel:

NIGHTLY THOUGHTS

Today I Chose To See: Today I Noticed A Positive Change In:

Today I Forgave: I Stopped Criticizing Myself And
                                        Started Saying:

Today I Expected: A Naturally Good Feeling Thought:

When I Got Or Did Not Get What I   When I Conversed With Someone
Expected, I: Who Was Feeling Bad About
                                        Themselves Or Complaining, I:

Today I Stretched My Beliefs By: A List Of Some Positive Thoughts I
                                        Had Today That I Did Not Oppose
                                        With Negative Thoughts:

A NEW BELIEF
MORNING THOUGHTS

Date: My Mood:

Today's Affirmation: Today I Am Releasing:

Today's New Beliefs: Today I Am Choosing To Feel:

NIGHTLY THOUGHTS

Today I Chose To See: Today I Noticed A Positive Change In:

Today I Forgave: I Stopped Criticizing Myself And
                                         Started Saying:

Today I Expected: A Naturally Good Feeling Thought:

When I Got Or Did Not Get What I   When I Conversed With Someone
Expected, I: Who Was Feeling Bad About
                                         Themselves Or Complaining, I:

Today I Stretched My Beliefs By: A List Of Some Positive Thoughts I
                                         Had Today That I Did Not Oppose
                                         With Negative Thoughts:

MY POSITIVE THOUGHTS

A NEW BELIEF
MORNING THOUGHTS

Date: My Mood:

Today's Affirmation: Today I Am Releasing:

Today's New Beliefs: Today I Am Choosing To Feel:

NIGHTLY THOUGHTS

Today I Chose To See: Today I Noticed A Positive Change In:

Today I Forgave: I Stopped Criticizing Myself And
                                         Started Saying:

Today I Expected: A Naturally Good Feeling Thought:

When I Got Or Did Not Get What I   When I Conversed With Someone
Expected, I: Who Was Feeling Bad About
                                         Themselves Or Complaining, I:

Today I Stretched My Beliefs By: A List Of Some Positive Thoughts I
                                         Had Today That I Did Not Oppose
                                         With Negative Thoughts:

I AM DOING MORE FOR MYSELF, BY MYSELF, AND I FEEL GOOD.

A NEW BELIEF
MORNING THOUGHTS

Date: My Mood:

Today's Affirmation: Today I Am Releasing:

Today's New Beliefs: Today I Am Choosing To Feel:

NIGHTLY THOUGHTS

Today I Chose To See: Today I Noticed A Positive Change In:

Today I Forgave: I Stopped Criticizing Myself And
                                        Started Saying:

Today I Expected: A Naturally Good Feeling Thought:

When I Got Or Did Not Get What I   When I Conversed With Someone
Expected, I: Who Was Feeling Bad About
                                        Themselves Or Complaining, I:

Today I Stretched My Beliefs By: A List Of Some Positive Thoughts I
                                        Had Today That I Did Not Oppose
                                        With Negative Thoughts:

SOMETIMES THE THOUGHT ALONE IS WHAT CAUSES MORE PAIN THEN THE ACTUAL ACT.

A NEW BELIEF
MORNING THOUGHTS

Date: My Mood:

Today's Affirmation: Today I Am Releasing:

Today's New Beliefs: Today I Am Choosing To Feel:

NIGHTLY THOUGHTS

Today I Chose To See: Today I Noticed A Positive Change In:

Today I Forgave: I Stopped Criticizing Myself And
                                           Started Saying:

Today I Expected: A Naturally Good Feeling Thought:

When I Got Or Did Not Get What I   When I Conversed With Someone
Expected, I: Who Was Feeling Bad About
                                           Themselves Or Complaining, I:

Today I Stretched My Beliefs By: A List Of Some Positive Thoughts I
                                           Had Today That I Did Not Oppose
                                           With Negative Thoughts:

GREAT THINGS ARE HAPPENING RIGHT NOW.

A NEW BELIEF
MORNING THOUGHTS

Date: My Mood:

Today's Affirmation: Today I Am Releasing:

Today's New Beliefs: Today I Am Choosing To Feel:

NIGHTLY THOUGHTS

Today I Chose To See: Today I Noticed A Positive Change In:

Today I Forgave: I Stopped Criticizing Myself And
                                         Started Saying:

Today I Expected: A Naturally Good Feeling Thought:

When I Got Or Did Not Get What I   When I Conversed With Someone
Expected, I: Who Was Feeling Bad About
                                         Themselves Or Complaining, I:

Today I Stretched My Beliefs By: A List Of Some Positive Thoughts I
                                         Had Today That I Did Not Oppose
                                         With Negative Thoughts:

A NEW BELIEF
MORNING THOUGHTS

Date: My Mood:

Today's Affirmation: Today I Am Releasing:

Today's New Beliefs: Today I Am Choosing To Feel:

NIGHTLY THOUGHTS

Today I Chose To See: Today I Noticed A Positive Change In:

Today I Forgave: I Stopped Criticizing Myself And
                                         Started Saying:

Today I Expected: A Naturally Good Feeling Thought:

When I Got Or Did Not Get What I   When I Conversed With Someone
Expected, I: Who Was Feeling Bad About
                                         Themselves Or Complaining, I:

Today I Stretched My Beliefs By: A List Of Some Positive Thoughts I
                                         Had Today That I Did Not Oppose
                                         With Negative Thoughts:

I AM GROWING AND MANIFESTING BECAUSE MY POSITIVE THOUGHTS HAVE GROWN MORE AND MORE POWERFUL.

MY POSITIVE THOUGHTS

A NEW BELIEF
MORNING THOUGHTS

Date: My Mood:

Today's Affirmation: Today I Am Releasing:

Today's New Beliefs: Today I Am Choosing To Feel:

NIGHTLY THOUGHTS

Today I Chose To See: Today I Noticed A Positive Change In:

Today I Forgave: I Stopped Criticizing Myself And
                                         Started Saying:

Today I Expected: A Naturally Good Feeling Thought:

When I Got Or Did Not Get What I   When I Conversed With Someone
Expected, I: Who Was Feeling Bad About
                                         Themselves Or Complaining, I:

Today I Stretched My Beliefs By: A List Of Some Positive Thoughts I
                                         Had Today That I Did Not Oppose
                                         With Negative Thoughts:

A NEW BELIEF
MORNING THOUGHTS

Date: My Mood:

Today's Affirmation: Today I Am Releasing:

Today's New Beliefs: Today I Am Choosing To Feel:

NIGHTLY THOUGHTS

Today I Chose To See: Today I Noticed A Positive Change In:

Today I Forgave: I Stopped Criticizing Myself And
                                     Started Saying:

Today I Expected: A Naturally Good Feeling Thought:

When I Got Or Did Not Get What I   When I Conversed With Someone
Expected, I: Who Was Feeling Bad About
                                     Themselves Or Complaining, I:

Today I Stretched My Beliefs By: A List Of Some Positive Thoughts I
                                     Had Today That I Did Not Oppose
                                     With Negative Thoughts:

A NEW BELIEF
MORNING THOUGHTS

Date: My Mood:

Today's Affirmation: Today I Am Releasing:

Today's New Beliefs: Today I Am Choosing To Feel:

NIGHTLY THOUGHTS

Today I Chose To See: Today I Noticed A Positive Change In:

Today I Forgave: I Stopped Criticizing Myself And
                                         Started Saying:

Today I Expected: A Naturally Good Feeling Thought:

When I Got Or Did Not Get What I   When I Conversed With Someone
Expected, I: Who Was Feeling Bad About
                                         Themselves Or Complaining, I:

Today I Stretched My Beliefs By: A List Of Some Positive Thoughts I
                                         Had Today That I Did Not Oppose
                                         With Negative Thoughts:

LIVING MORE WORRYING LESS.

A NEW BELIEF
<u>MORNING THOUGHTS</u>

Date:

Today's Affirmation:

Today's New Beliefs:

My Mood:

Today I Am Releasing:

Today I Am Choosing To Feel:

<u>NIGHTLY THOUGHTS</u>

Today I Chose To See:

Today I Forgave:

Today I Expected:

When I Got Or Did Not Get What I
Expected, I:

Today I Stretched My Beliefs By:

Today I Noticed A Positive Change In:

I Stopped Criticizing Myself And
Started Saying:

A Naturally Good Feeling Thought:

When I Conversed With Someone
Who Was Feeling Bad About
Themselves Or Complaining, I:

A List Of Some Positive Thoughts I
Had Today That I Did Not Oppose
With Negative Thoughts:

A NEW BELIEF
MORNING THOUGHTS

Date: My Mood:

Today's Affirmation: Today I Am Releasing:

Today's New Beliefs: Today I Am Choosing To Feel:

NIGHTLY THOUGHTS

Today I Chose To See: Today I Noticed A Positive Change In:

Today I Forgave: I Stopped Criticizing Myself And
                                        Started Saying:

Today I Expected: A Naturally Good Feeling Thought:

When I Got Or Did Not Get What I   When I Conversed With Someone
Expected, I: Who Was Feeling Bad About
                                        Themselves Or Complaining, I:

Today I Stretched My Beliefs By: A List Of Some Positive Thoughts I
                                        Had Today That I Did Not Oppose
                                        With Negative Thoughts:

A NEW BELIEF
MORNING THOUGHTS

Date: My Mood:

Today's Affirmation: Today I Am Releasing:

Today's New Beliefs: Today I Am Choosing To Feel:

NIGHTLY THOUGHTS

Today I Chose To See: Today I Noticed A Positive Change In:

Today I Forgave: I Stopped Criticizing Myself And
                                         Started Saying:

Today I Expected: A Naturally Good Feeling Thought:

When I Got Or Did Not Get What I   When I Conversed With Someone
Expected, I: Who Was Feeling Bad About
                                         Themselves Or Complaining, I:

Today I Stretched My Beliefs By: A List Of Some Positive Thoughts I
                                         Had Today That I Did Not Oppose
                                         With Negative Thoughts:

MY POSITIVE THOUGHTS

A NEW BELIEF
<u>MORNING THOUGHTS</u>

Date: My Mood:

Today's Affirmation: Today I Am Releasing:

Today's New Beliefs: Today I Am Choosing To Feel:

<u>NIGHTLY THOUGHTS</u>

Today I Chose To See: Today I Noticed A Positive Change In:

Today I Forgave: I Stopped Criticizing Myself And
                                Started Saying:

Today I Expected: A Naturally Good Feeling Thought:

When I Got Or Did Not Get What I   When I Conversed With Someone
Expected, I: Who Was Feeling Bad About
                                Themselves Or Complaining, I:

Today I Stretched My Beliefs By: A List Of Some Positive Thoughts I
                                Had Today That I Did Not Oppose
                                With Negative Thoughts:

A NEW BELIEF
MORNING THOUGHTS

Date: My Mood:

Today's Affirmation: Today I Am Releasing:

Today's New Beliefs: Today I Am Choosing To Feel:

NIGHTLY THOUGHTS

Today I Chose To See: Today I Noticed A Positive Change In:

Today I Forgave: I Stopped Criticizing Myself And
                                         Started Saying:

Today I Expected: A Naturally Good Feeling Thought:

When I Got Or Did Not Get What I   When I Conversed With Someone
Expected, I: Who Was Feeling Bad About
                                         Themselves Or Complaining, I:

Today I Stretched My Beliefs By: A List Of Some Positive Thoughts I
                                         Had Today That I Did Not Oppose
                                         With Negative Thoughts:

EVERYDAY I AM MAKING AMAZING DECISIONS THAT WILL CHANGE MY LIFE.

POSITIVE THOUGHTS = MORE PEACE.

A NEW BELIEF
MORNING THOUGHTS

Date: My Mood:

Today's Affirmation: Today I Am Releasing:

Today's New Beliefs: Today I Am Choosing To Feel:

NIGHTLY THOUGHTS

Today I Chose To See: Today I Noticed A Positive Change In:

Today I Forgave: I Stopped Criticizing Myself And
                                         Started Saying:

Today I Expected: A Naturally Good Feeling Thought:

When I Got Or Did Not Get What I   When I Conversed With Someone
Expected, I: Who Was Feeling Bad About
                                         Themselves Or Complaining, I:

Today I Stretched My Beliefs By: A List Of Some Positive Thoughts I
                                         Had Today That I Did Not Oppose
                                         With Negative Thoughts:

A NEW BELIEF
MORNING THOUGHTS

Date: My Mood:

Today's Affirmation: Today I Am Releasing:

Today's New Beliefs: Today I Am Choosing To Feel:

NIGHTLY THOUGHTS

Today I Chose To See: Today I Noticed A Positive Change In:

Today I Forgave: I Stopped Criticizing Myself And
                                   Started Saying:

Today I Expected: A Naturally Good Feeling Thought:

When I Got Or Did Not Get What I   When I Conversed With Someone
Expected, I: Who Was Feeling Bad About
                                   Themselves Or Complaining, I:

Today I Stretched My Beliefs By: A List Of Some Positive Thoughts I
                                   Had Today That I Did Not Oppose
                                   With Negative Thoughts:

I TRUST GOD.

NO NEGATIVE THOUGHT ABOUT ME SHALL PROSPER.

A NEW BELIEF
MORNING THOUGHTS

Date: My Mood:

Today's Affirmation: Today I Am Releasing:

Today's New Beliefs: Today I Am Choosing To Feel:

NIGHTLY THOUGHTS

Today I Chose To See: Today I Noticed A Positive Change In:

Today I Forgave: I Stopped Criticizing Myself And
                                        Started Saying:

Today I Expected: A Naturally Good Feeling Thought:

When I Got Or Did Not Get What I   When I Conversed With Someone
Expected, I: Who Was Feeling Bad About
                                        Themselves Or Complaining, I:

Today I Stretched My Beliefs By: A List Of Some Positive Thoughts I
                                        Had Today That I Did Not Oppose
                                        With Negative Thoughts:

A NEW BELIEF
MORNING THOUGHTS

Date: My Mood:

Today's Affirmation: Today I Am Releasing:

Today's New Beliefs: Today I Am Choosing To Feel:

NIGHTLY THOUGHTS

Today I Chose To See: Today I Noticed A Positive Change In:

Today I Forgave: I Stopped Criticizing Myself And
                                     Started Saying:

Today I Expected: A Naturally Good Feeling Thought:

When I Got Or Did Not Get What I   When I Conversed With Someone
Expected, I: Who Was Feeling Bad About
                                     Themselves Or Complaining, I:

Today I Stretched My Beliefs By: A List Of Some Positive Thoughts I
                                     Had Today That I Did Not Oppose
                                     With Negative Thoughts:

A NEW BELIEF
MORNING THOUGHTS

Date: My Mood:

Today's Affirmation: Today I Am Releasing:

Today's New Beliefs: Today I Am Choosing To Feel:

NIGHTLY THOUGHTS

Today I Chose To See: Today I Noticed A Positive Change In:

Today I Forgave: I Stopped Criticizing Myself And
                                     Started Saying:

Today I Expected: A Naturally Good Feeling Thought:

When I Got Or Did Not Get What I   When I Conversed With Someone
Expected, I: Who Was Feeling Bad About
                                     Themselves Or Complaining, I:

Today I Stretched My Beliefs By: A List Of Some Positive Thoughts I
                                     Had Today That I Did Not Oppose
                                     With Negative Thoughts:

MY POSITIVE THOUGHTS

I LIKE TO REMEMBER HOW BLESSED I AM.

A NEW BELIEF
MORNING THOUGHTS

Date: My Mood:

Today's Affirmation: Today I Am Releasing:

Today's New Beliefs: Today I Am Choosing To Feel:

NIGHTLY THOUGHTS

Today I Chose To See: Today I Noticed A Positive Change In:

Today I Forgave: I Stopped Criticizing Myself And
                                        Started Saying:

Today I Expected: A Naturally Good Feeling Thought:

When I Got Or Did Not Get What I   When I Conversed With Someone
Expected, I: Who Was Feeling Bad About
                                        Themselves Or Complaining, I:

Today I Stretched My Beliefs By: A List Of Some Positive Thoughts I
                                        Had Today That I Did Not Oppose
                                        With Negative Thoughts:

A NEW BELIEF
MORNING THOUGHTS

Date: My Mood:

Today's Affirmation: Today I Am Releasing:

Today's New Beliefs: Today I Am Choosing To Feel:

NIGHTLY THOUGHTS

Today I Chose To See: Today I Noticed A Positive Change In:

Today I Forgave: I Stopped Criticizing Myself And
                                         Started Saying:

Today I Expected: A Naturally Good Feeling Thought:

When I Got Or Did Not Get What I   When I Conversed With Someone
Expected, I: Who Was Feeling Bad About
                                         Themselves Or Complaining, I:

Today I Stretched My Beliefs By: A List Of Some Positive Thoughts I
                                         Had Today That I Did Not Oppose
                                         With Negative Thoughts:

MY POSITIVE THOUGHTS

ATTITUDE DETERMINES DIRECTION.

A NEW BELIEF
MORNING THOUGHTS

Date: My Mood:

Today's Affirmation: Today I Am Releasing:

Today's New Beliefs: Today I Am Choosing To Feel:

NIGHTLY THOUGHTS

Today I Chose To See: Today I Noticed A Positive Change In:

Today I Forgave: I Stopped Criticizing Myself And
                                     Started Saying:

Today I Expected: A Naturally Good Feeling Thought:

When I Got Or Did Not Get What I   When I Conversed With Someone
Expected, I: Who Was Feeling Bad About
                                     Themselves Or Complaining, I:

Today I Stretched My Beliefs By: A List Of Some Positive Thoughts I
                                     Had Today That I Did Not Oppose
                                     With Negative Thoughts:

I WILL START AND END EACH DAY WITH A POSITIVE ATTITUDE.

A NEW BELIEF
<u>MORNING THOUGHTS</u>

Date: My Mood:

Today's Affirmation: Today I Am Releasing:

Today's New Beliefs: Today I Am Choosing To Feel:

<u>NIGHTLY THOUGHTS</u>

Today I Chose To See: Today I Noticed A Positive Change In:

Today I Forgave: I Stopped Criticizing Myself And
                                         Started Saying:

Today I Expected: A Naturally Good Feeling Thought:

When I Got Or Did Not Get What I   When I Conversed With Someone
Expected, I: Who Was Feeling Bad About
                                         Themselves Or Complaining, I:

Today I Stretched My Beliefs By: A List Of Some Positive Thoughts I
                                         Had Today That I Did Not Oppose
                                         With Negative Thoughts:

A NEW BELIEF
MORNING THOUGHTS

Date: My Mood:

Today's Affirmation: Today I Am Releasing:

Today's New Beliefs: Today I Am Choosing To Feel:

NIGHTLY THOUGHTS

Today I Chose To See: Today I Noticed A Positive Change In:

Today I Forgave: I Stopped Criticizing Myself And
                                         Started Saying:

Today I Expected: A Naturally Good Feeling Thought:

When I Got Or Did Not Get What I   When I Conversed With Someone
Expected, I: Who Was Feeling Bad About
                                         Themselves Or Complaining, I:

Today I Stretched My Beliefs By: A List Of Some Positive Thoughts I
                                         Had Today That I Did Not Oppose
                                         With Negative Thoughts:

NEGATIVE THOUGHTS COME FROM FEAR, REGRET, AND DISBELIEF. I WILL NO LONGER LIVE THIS WAY.

THE MORE THAT I CHOOSE TO FEEL GOOD THE MORE I WILL BE SURROUNDED BY THINGS THAT WILL CONTINUE TO MAKE ME FEEL GOOD.

A NEW BELIEF
MORNING THOUGHTS

Date: My Mood:

Today's Affirmation: Today I Am Releasing:

Today's New Beliefs: Today I Am Choosing To Feel:

NIGHTLY THOUGHTS

Today I Chose To See: Today I Noticed A Positive Change In:

Today I Forgave: I Stopped Criticizing Myself And
                                Started Saying:

Today I Expected: A Naturally Good Feeling Thought:

When I Got Or Did Not Get What I   When I Conversed With Someone
Expected, I: Who Was Feeling Bad About
                                    Themselves Or Complaining, I:

Today I Stretched My Beliefs By: A List Of Some Positive Thoughts I
                                    Had Today That I Did Not Oppose
                                    With Negative Thoughts:

A NEW BELIEF
MORNING THOUGHTS

Date: My Mood:

Today's Affirmation: Today I Am Releasing:

Today's New Beliefs: Today I Am Choosing To Feel:

NIGHTLY THOUGHTS

Today I Chose To See: Today I Noticed A Positive Change In:

Today I Forgave: I Stopped Criticizing Myself And
                                    Started Saying:

Today I Expected: A Naturally Good Feeling Thought:

When I Got Or Did Not Get What I   When I Conversed With Someone
Expected, I: Who Was Feeling Bad About
                                    Themselves Or Complaining, I:

Today I Stretched My Beliefs By: A List Of Some Positive Thoughts I
                                    Had Today That I Did Not Oppose
                                    With Negative Thoughts:

A NEW BELIEF
MORNING THOUGHTS

Date: My Mood:

Today's Affirmation: Today I Am Releasing:

Today's New Beliefs: Today I Am Choosing To Feel:

NIGHTLY THOUGHTS

Today I Chose To See: Today I Noticed A Positive Change In:

Today I Forgave: I Stopped Criticizing Myself And
                                         Started Saying:

Today I Expected: A Naturally Good Feeling Thought:

When I Got Or Did Not Get What I   When I Conversed With Someone
Expected, I: Who Was Feeling Bad About
                                         Themselves Or Complaining, I:

Today I Stretched My Beliefs By: A List Of Some Positive Thoughts I
                                         Had Today That I Did Not Oppose
                                         With Negative Thoughts:

I THINK I CAN.
I THINK I CAN.
I KNOW I CAN.

MY POSITIVE THOUGHTS

A NEW BELIEF
MORNING THOUGHTS

Date: My Mood:

Today's Affirmation: Today I Am Releasing:

Today's New Beliefs: Today I Am Choosing To Feel:

NIGHTLY THOUGHTS

Today I Chose To See: Today I Noticed A Positive Change In:

Today I Forgave: I Stopped Criticizing Myself And
                                           Started Saying:

Today I Expected: A Naturally Good Feeling Thought:

When I Got Or Did Not Get What I   When I Conversed With Someone
Expected, I: Who Was Feeling Bad About
                                           Themselves Or Complaining, I:

Today I Stretched My Beliefs By: A List Of Some Positive Thoughts I
                                           Had Today That I Did Not Oppose
                                           With Negative Thoughts:

A NEW BELIEF
MORNING THOUGHTS

Date: My Mood:

Today's Affirmation: Today I Am Releasing:

Today's New Beliefs: Today I Am Choosing To Feel:

NIGHTLY THOUGHTS

Today I Chose To See: Today I Noticed A Positive Change In:

Today I Forgave: I Stopped Criticizing Myself And
                                   Started Saying:

Today I Expected: A Naturally Good Feeling Thought:

When I Got Or Did Not Get What I   When I Conversed With Someone
Expected, I: Who Was Feeling Bad About
                                   Themselves Or Complaining, I:

Today I Stretched My Beliefs By: A List Of Some Positive Thoughts I
                                   Had Today That I Did Not Oppose
                                   With Negative Thoughts:

A NEW BELIEF
MORNING THOUGHTS

Date: My Mood:

Today's Affirmation: Today I Am Releasing:

Today's New Beliefs: Today I Am Choosing To Feel:

NIGHTLY THOUGHTS

Today I Chose To See: Today I Noticed A Positive Change In:

Today I Forgave: I Stopped Criticizing Myself And
                                     Started Saying:

Today I Expected: A Naturally Good Feeling Thought:

When I Got Or Did Not Get What I   When I Conversed With Someone
Expected, I: Who Was Feeling Bad About
                                     Themselves Or Complaining, I:

Today I Stretched My Beliefs By: A List Of Some Positive Thoughts I
                                     Had Today That I Did Not Oppose
                                     With Negative Thoughts:

I SEE POSITIVE RESULTS BECAUSE IT FIRST STARTED WITH POSITIVE THOUGHTS.

A NEW BELIEF
MORNING THOUGHTS

Date: My Mood:

Today's Affirmation: Today I Am Releasing:

Today's New Beliefs: Today I Am Choosing To Feel:

NIGHTLY THOUGHTS

Today I Chose To See: Today I Noticed A Positive Change In:

Today I Forgave: I Stopped Criticizing Myself And
                                         Started Saying:

Today I Expected: A Naturally Good Feeling Thought:

When I Got Or Did Not Get What I   When I Conversed With Someone
Expected, I: Who Was Feeling Bad About
                                         Themselves Or Complaining, I:

Today I Stretched My Beliefs By: A List Of Some Positive Thoughts I
                                         Had Today That I Did Not Oppose
                                         With Negative Thoughts:

TAKING CARE OF MYSELF. MIND. BODY. SPIRIT.

A NEW BELIEF
MORNING THOUGHTS

Date: My Mood:

Today's Affirmation: Today I Am Releasing:

Today's New Beliefs: Today I Am Choosing To Feel:

NIGHTLY THOUGHTS

Today I Chose To See: Today I Noticed A Positive Change In:

Today I Forgave: I Stopped Criticizing Myself And
                                Started Saying:

Today I Expected: A Naturally Good Feeling Thought:

When I Got Or Did Not Get What I   When I Conversed With Someone
Expected, I: Who Was Feeling Bad About
                                Themselves Or Complaining, I:

Today I Stretched My Beliefs By: A List Of Some Positive Thoughts I
                                Had Today That I Did Not Oppose
                                With Negative Thoughts:

A NEW BELIEF
MORNING THOUGHTS

Date: My Mood:

Today's Affirmation: Today I Am Releasing:

Today's New Beliefs: Today I Am Choosing To Feel:

NIGHTLY THOUGHTS

Today I Chose To See: Today I Noticed A Positive Change In:

Today I Forgave: I Stopped Criticizing Myself And
                                        Started Saying:

Today I Expected: A Naturally Good Feeling Thought:

When I Got Or Did Not Get What I   When I Conversed With Someone
Expected, I: Who Was Feeling Bad About
                                        Themselves Or Complaining, I:

Today I Stretched My Beliefs By: A List Of Some Positive Thoughts I
                                        Had Today That I Did Not Oppose
                                        With Negative Thoughts:

A NEW BELIEF
MORNING THOUGHTS

Date: My Mood:

Today's Affirmation: Today I Am Releasing:

Today's New Beliefs: Today I Am Choosing To Feel:

NIGHTLY THOUGHTS

Today I Chose To See: Today I Noticed A Positive Change In:

Today I Forgave: I Stopped Criticizing Myself And
                                    Started Saying:

Today I Expected: A Naturally Good Feeling Thought:

When I Got Or Did Not Get What I   When I Conversed With Someone
Expected, I: Who Was Feeling Bad About
                                    Themselves Or Complaining, I:

Today I Stretched My Beliefs By: A List Of Some Positive Thoughts I
                                    Had Today That I Did Not Oppose
                                    With Negative Thoughts:

DREAMS COME TRUE WITH POSITIVE ATTITUDES.

IT REALLY IS THE LITTLE THINGS IN LIFE.

A NEW BELIEF
MORNING THOUGHTS

Date: My Mood:

Today's Affirmation: Today I Am Releasing:

Today's New Beliefs: Today I Am Choosing To Feel:

NIGHTLY THOUGHTS

Today I Chose To See: Today I Noticed A Positive Change In:

Today I Forgave: I Stopped Criticizing Myself And
                                         Started Saying:

Today I Expected: A Naturally Good Feeling Thought:

When I Got Or Did Not Get What I   When I Conversed With Someone
Expected, I: Who Was Feeling Bad About
                                         Themselves Or Complaining, I:

Today I Stretched My Beliefs By: A List Of Some Positive Thoughts I
                                         Had Today That I Did Not Oppose
                                         With Negative Thoughts:

A NEW BELIEF
MORNING THOUGHTS

Date: My Mood:

Today's Affirmation: Today I Am Releasing:

Today's New Beliefs: Today I Am Choosing To Feel:

NIGHTLY THOUGHTS

Today I Chose To See: Today I Noticed A Positive Change In:

Today I Forgave: I Stopped Criticizing Myself And
                                     Started Saying:

Today I Expected: A Naturally Good Feeling Thought:

When I Got Or Did Not Get What I   When I Conversed With Someone
Expected, I: Who Was Feeling Bad About
                                     Themselves Or Complaining, I:

Today I Stretched My Beliefs By: A List Of Some Positive Thoughts I
                                     Had Today That I Did Not Oppose
                                     With Negative Thoughts:

A NEW BELIEF
MORNING THOUGHTS

Date: My Mood:

Today's Affirmation: Today I Am Releasing:

Today's New Beliefs: Today I Am Choosing To Feel:

NIGHTLY THOUGHTS

Today I Chose To See: Today I Noticed A Positive Change In:

Today I Forgave: I Stopped Criticizing Myself And
                                         Started Saying:

Today I Expected: A Naturally Good Feeling Thought:

When I Got Or Did Not Get What I   When I Conversed With Someone
Expected, I: Who Was Feeling Bad About
                                         Themselves Or Complaining, I:

Today I Stretched My Beliefs By: A List Of Some Positive Thoughts I
                                         Had Today That I Did Not Oppose
                                         With Negative Thoughts:

INSECURITIES WILL NOT STOP ME FROM BEING MY BEST SELF.

MY POSITIVE THOUGHTS

A NEW BELIEF
MORNING THOUGHTS

Date: My Mood:

Today's Affirmation: Today I Am Releasing:

Today's New Beliefs: Today I Am Choosing To Feel:

NIGHTLY THOUGHTS

Today I Chose To See: Today I Noticed A Positive Change In:

Today I Forgave: I Stopped Criticizing Myself And
                                Started Saying:

Today I Expected: A Naturally Good Feeling Thought:

When I Got Or Did Not Get What I   When I Conversed With Someone
Expected, I: Who Was Feeling Bad About
                                    Themselves Or Complaining, I:

Today I Stretched My Beliefs By: A List Of Some Positive Thoughts I
                                    Had Today That I Did Not Oppose
                                    With Negative Thoughts:

A NEW BELIEF
MORNING THOUGHTS

Date: My Mood:

Today's Affirmation: Today I Am Releasing:

Today's New Beliefs: Today I Am Choosing To Feel:

NIGHTLY THOUGHTS

Today I Chose To See: Today I Noticed A Positive Change In:

Today I Forgave: I Stopped Criticizing Myself And
                                         Started Saying:

Today I Expected: A Naturally Good Feeling Thought:

When I Got Or Did Not Get What I   When I Conversed With Someone
Expected, I: Who Was Feeling Bad About
                                         Themselves Or Complaining, I:

Today I Stretched My Beliefs By: A List Of Some Positive Thoughts I
                                         Had Today That I Did Not Oppose
                                         With Negative Thoughts:

A NEW BELIEF
MORNING THOUGHTS

Date: My Mood:

Today's Affirmation: Today I Am Releasing:

Today's New Beliefs: Today I Am Choosing To Feel:

NIGHTLY THOUGHTS

Today I Chose To See: Today I Noticed A Positive Change In:

Today I Forgave: I Stopped Criticizing Myself And
                                   Started Saying:

Today I Expected: A Naturally Good Feeling Thought:

When I Got Or Did Not Get What I   When I Conversed With Someone
Expected, I: Who Was Feeling Bad About
                                   Themselves Or Complaining, I:

Today I Stretched My Beliefs By: A List Of Some Positive Thoughts I
                                   Had Today That I Did Not Oppose
                                   With Negative Thoughts:

THE BEST THINGS ARE HAPPENING TO ME RIGHT NOW.

I AM
EVERYTHING
GOD SAYS
I AM.

A NEW BELIEF
MORNING THOUGHTS

Date: My Mood:

Today's Affirmation: Today I Am Releasing:

Today's New Beliefs: Today I Am Choosing To Feel:

NIGHTLY THOUGHTS

Today I Chose To See: Today I Noticed A Positive Change In:

Today I Forgave: I Stopped Criticizing Myself And
                                     Started Saying:

Today I Expected: A Naturally Good Feeling Thought:

When I Got Or Did Not Get What I   When I Conversed With Someone
Expected, I: Who Was Feeling Bad About
                                     Themselves Or Complaining, I:

Today I Stretched My Beliefs By: A List Of Some Positive Thoughts I
                                     Had Today That I Did Not Oppose
                                     With Negative Thoughts:

A NEW BELIEF
MORNING THOUGHTS

Date: My Mood:

Today's Affirmation: Today I Am Releasing:

Today's New Beliefs: Today I Am Choosing To Feel:

NIGHTLY THOUGHTS

Today I Chose To See: Today I Noticed A Positive Change In:

Today I Forgave: I Stopped Criticizing Myself And
                                Started Saying:

Today I Expected: A Naturally Good Feeling Thought:

When I Got Or Did Not Get What I   When I Conversed With Someone
Expected, I: Who Was Feeling Bad About
                                    Themselves Or Complaining, I:

Today I Stretched My Beliefs By: A List Of Some Positive Thoughts I
                                    Had Today That I Did Not Oppose
                                    With Negative Thoughts:

A NEW BELIEF
MORNING THOUGHTS

Date: My Mood:

Today's Affirmation: Today I Am Releasing:

Today's New Beliefs: Today I Am Choosing To Feel:

NIGHTLY THOUGHTS

Today I Chose To See: Today I Noticed A Positive Change In:

Today I Forgave: I Stopped Criticizing Myself And
                                         Started Saying:

Today I Expected: A Naturally Good Feeling Thought:

When I Got Or Did Not Get What I   When I Conversed With Someone
Expected, I: Who Was Feeling Bad About
                                         Themselves Or Complaining, I:

Today I Stretched My Beliefs By: A List Of Some Positive Thoughts I
                                         Had Today That I Did Not Oppose
                                         With Negative Thoughts:

MY POSITIVE THOUGHTS

A NEW BELIEF
MORNING THOUGHTS

Date: My Mood:

Today's Affirmation: Today I Am Releasing:

Today's New Beliefs: Today I Am Choosing To Feel:

NIGHTLY THOUGHTS

Today I Chose To See: Today I Noticed A Positive Change In:

Today I Forgave: I Stopped Criticizing Myself And
                                               Started Saying:

Today I Expected: A Naturally Good Feeling Thought:

When I Got Or Did Not Get What I   When I Conversed With Someone
Expected, I: Who Was Feeling Bad About
                                               Themselves Or Complaining, I:

Today I Stretched My Beliefs By: A List Of Some Positive Thoughts I
                                               Had Today That I Did Not Oppose
                                               With Negative Thoughts:

A NEW BELIEF
MORNING THOUGHTS

Date: My Mood:

Today's Affirmation: Today I Am Releasing:

Today's New Beliefs: Today I Am Choosing To Feel:

NIGHTLY THOUGHTS

Today I Chose To See: Today I Noticed A Positive Change In:

Today I Forgave: I Stopped Criticizing Myself And
                                         Started Saying:

Today I Expected: A Naturally Good Feeling Thought:

When I Got Or Did Not Get What I   When I Conversed With Someone
Expected, I: Who Was Feeling Bad About
                                         Themselves Or Complaining, I:

Today I Stretched My Beliefs By: A List Of Some Positive Thoughts I
                                         Had Today That I Did Not Oppose
                                         With Negative Thoughts:

I ONLY WANT WHAT GOD SAYS IS MINE.

A NEW BELIEF
MORNING THOUGHTS

Date: My Mood:

Today's Affirmation: Today I Am Releasing:

Today's New Beliefs: Today I Am Choosing To Feel:

NIGHTLY THOUGHTS

Today I Chose To See: Today I Noticed A Positive Change In:

Today I Forgave: I Stopped Criticizing Myself And
                                         Started Saying:

Today I Expected: A Naturally Good Feeling Thought:

When I Got Or Did Not Get What I   When I Conversed With Someone
Expected, I: Who Was Feeling Bad About
                                         Themselves Or Complaining, I:

Today I Stretched My Beliefs By: A List Of Some Positive Thoughts I
                                         Had Today That I Did Not Oppose
                                         With Negative Thoughts:

A NEW BELIEF
MORNING THOUGHTS

Date: My Mood:

Today's Affirmation: Today I Am Releasing:

Today's New Beliefs: Today I Am Choosing To Feel:

NIGHTLY THOUGHTS

Today I Chose To See: Today I Noticed A Positive Change In:

Today I Forgave: I Stopped Criticizing Myself And
                                Started Saying:

Today I Expected: A Naturally Good Feeling Thought:

When I Got Or Did Not Get What I   When I Conversed With Someone
Expected, I: Who Was Feeling Bad About
                                Themselves Or Complaining, I:

Today I Stretched My Beliefs By: A List Of Some Positive Thoughts I
                                Had Today That I Did Not Oppose
                                With Negative Thoughts:

A NEW BELIEF
MORNING THOUGHTS

Date: My Mood:

Today's Affirmation: Today I Am Releasing:

Today's New Beliefs: Today I Am Choosing To Feel:

NIGHTLY THOUGHTS

Today I Chose To See: Today I Noticed A Positive Change In:

Today I Forgave: I Stopped Criticizing Myself And
                                         Started Saying:

Today I Expected: A Naturally Good Feeling Thought:

When I Got Or Did Not Get What I   When I Conversed With Someone
Expected, I: Who Was Feeling Bad About
                                         Themselves Or Complaining, I:

Today I Stretched My Beliefs By: A List Of Some Positive Thoughts I
                                         Had Today That I Did Not Oppose
                                         With Negative Thoughts:

MY POSITIVE THOUGHTS

I WILL ONLY. BELIEVE IN THE GOOD.

A NEW BELIEF
MORNING THOUGHTS

Date: My Mood:

Today's Affirmation: Today I Am Releasing:

Today's New Beliefs: Today I Am Choosing To Feel:

NIGHTLY THOUGHTS

Today I Chose To See: Today I Noticed A Positive Change In:

Today I Forgave: I Stopped Criticizing Myself And
                                         Started Saying:

Today I Expected: A Naturally Good Feeling Thought:

When I Got Or Did Not Get What I   When I Conversed With Someone
Expected, I: Who Was Feeling Bad About
                                         Themselves Or Complaining, I:

Today I Stretched My Beliefs By: A List Of Some Positive Thoughts I
                                         Had Today That I Did Not Oppose
                                         With Negative Thoughts:

A NEW BELIEF
MORNING THOUGHTS

Date: My Mood:

Today's Affirmation: Today I Am Releasing:

Today's New Beliefs: Today I Am Choosing To Feel:

NIGHTLY THOUGHTS

Today I Chose To See: Today I Noticed A Positive Change In:

Today I Forgave: I Stopped Criticizing Myself And
                                         Started Saying:

Today I Expected: A Naturally Good Feeling Thought:

When I Got Or Did Not Get What I   When I Conversed With Someone
Expected, I: Who Was Feeling Bad About
                                         Themselves Or Complaining, I:

Today I Stretched My Beliefs By: A List Of Some Positive Thoughts I
                                         Had Today That I Did Not Oppose
                                         With Negative Thoughts:

A NEW BELIEF
MORNING THOUGHTS

Date: My Mood:

Today's Affirmation: Today I Am Releasing:

Today's New Beliefs: Today I Am Choosing To Feel:

NIGHTLY THOUGHTS

Today I Chose To See: Today I Noticed A Positive Change In:

Today I Forgave: I Stopped Criticizing Myself And
                                         Started Saying:

Today I Expected: A Naturally Good Feeling Thought:

When I Got Or Did Not Get What I   When I Conversed With Someone
Expected, I: Who Was Feeling Bad About
                                         Themselves Or Complaining, I:

Today I Stretched My Beliefs By: A List Of Some Positive Thoughts I
                                         Had Today That I Did Not Oppose
                                         With Negative Thoughts:

MY POSITIVE THOUGHTS

A NEW BELIEF
MORNING THOUGHTS

Date: My Mood:

Today's Affirmation: Today I Am Releasing:

Today's New Beliefs: Today I Am Choosing To Feel:

NIGHTLY THOUGHTS

Today I Chose To See: Today I Noticed A Positive Change In:

Today I Forgave: I Stopped Criticizing Myself And
                                         Started Saying:

Today I Expected: A Naturally Good Feeling Thought:

When I Got Or Did Not Get What I   When I Conversed With Someone
Expected, I: Who Was Feeling Bad About
                                         Themselves Or Complaining, I:

Today I Stretched My Beliefs By: A List Of Some Positive Thoughts I
                                         Had Today That I Did Not Oppose
                                         With Negative Thoughts:

A NEW BELIEF
MORNING THOUGHTS

Date: My Mood:

Today's Affirmation: Today I Am Releasing:

Today's New Beliefs: Today I Am Choosing To Feel:

NIGHTLY THOUGHTS

Today I Chose To See: Today I Noticed A Positive Change In:

Today I Forgave: I Stopped Criticizing Myself And
                                   Started Saying:

Today I Expected: A Naturally Good Feeling Thought:

When I Got Or Did Not Get What I   When I Conversed With Someone
Expected, I: Who Was Feeling Bad About
                                   Themselves Or Complaining, I:

Today I Stretched My Beliefs By: A List Of Some Positive Thoughts I
                                   Had Today That I Did Not Oppose
                                   With Negative Thoughts:

A NEW BELIEF
MORNING THOUGHTS

Date: My Mood:

Today's Affirmation: Today I Am Releasing:

Today's New Beliefs: Today I Am Choosing To Feel:

NIGHTLY THOUGHTS

Today I Chose To See: Today I Noticed A Positive Change In:

Today I Forgave: I Stopped Criticizing Myself And
                                           Started Saying:

Today I Expected: A Naturally Good Feeling Thought:

When I Got Or Did Not Get What I   When I Conversed With Someone
Expected, I: Who Was Feeling Bad About
                                           Themselves Or Complaining, I:

Today I Stretched My Beliefs By: A List Of Some Positive Thoughts I
                                           Had Today That I Did Not Oppose
                                           With Negative Thoughts:

OKAY, I HAVE MADE MISTAKES BUT I WILL STILL CONTINUE TO TRY MY BEST.

I AM PROUD OF WHO I AM.

A NEW BELIEF
MORNING THOUGHTS

Date: My Mood:

Today's Affirmation: Today I Am Releasing:

Today's New Beliefs: Today I Am Choosing To Feel:

NIGHTLY THOUGHTS

Today I Chose To See: Today I Noticed A Positive Change In:

Today I Forgave: I Stopped Criticizing Myself And
                                         Started Saying:

Today I Expected: A Naturally Good Feeling Thought:

When I Got Or Did Not Get What I   When I Conversed With Someone
Expected, I: Who Was Feeling Bad About
                                         Themselves Or Complaining, I:

Today I Stretched My Beliefs By: A List Of Some Positive Thoughts I
                                         Had Today That I Did Not Oppose
                                         With Negative Thoughts:

A NEW BELIEF
MORNING THOUGHTS

Date: My Mood:

Today's Affirmation: Today I Am Releasing:

Today's New Beliefs: Today I Am Choosing To Feel:

NIGHTLY THOUGHTS

Today I Chose To See: Today I Noticed A Positive Change In:

Today I Forgave: I Stopped Criticizing Myself And
                                         Started Saying:

Today I Expected: A Naturally Good Feeling Thought:

When I Got Or Did Not Get What I   When I Conversed With Someone
Expected, I: Who Was Feeling Bad About
                                         Themselves Or Complaining, I:

Today I Stretched My Beliefs By: A List Of Some Positive Thoughts I
                                         Had Today That I Did Not Oppose
                                         With Negative Thoughts:

A NEW BELIEF
MORNING THOUGHTS

Date: My Mood:

Today's Affirmation: Today I Am Releasing:

Today's New Beliefs: Today I Am Choosing To Feel:

NIGHTLY THOUGHTS

Today I Chose To See: Today I Noticed A Positive Change In:

Today I Forgave: I Stopped Criticizing Myself And
                                           Started Saying:

Today I Expected: A Naturally Good Feeling Thought:

When I Got Or Did Not Get What I   When I Conversed With Someone
Expected, I: Who Was Feeling Bad About
                                           Themselves Or Complaining, I:

Today I Stretched My Beliefs By: A List Of Some Positive Thoughts I
                                           Had Today That I Did Not Oppose
                                           With Negative Thoughts:

A NEW BELIEF
MORNING THOUGHTS

Date:

My Mood:

Today's Affirmation:

Today I Am Releasing:

Today's New Beliefs:

Today I Am Choosing To Feel:

NIGHTLY THOUGHTS

Today I Chose To See:

Today I Noticed A Positive Change In:

Today I Forgave:

I Stopped Criticizing Myself And Started Saying:

Today I Expected:

A Naturally Good Feeling Thought:

When I Got Or Did Not Get What I Expected, I:

When I Conversed With Someone Who Was Feeling Bad About Themselves Or Complaining, I:

Today I Stretched My Beliefs By:

A List Of Some Positive Thoughts I Had Today That I Did Not Oppose With Negative Thoughts:

I WILL NOT ALLOW FEAR TO TELL ME HOW TO LIVE MY LIFE.

GOD WILL NEVER GIVE UP ON ME.

A NEW BELIEF
MORNING THOUGHTS

Date: My Mood:

Today's Affirmation: Today I Am Releasing:

Today's New Beliefs: Today I Am Choosing To Feel:

NIGHTLY THOUGHTS

Today I Chose To See: Today I Noticed A Positive Change In:

Today I Forgave: I Stopped Criticizing Myself And
                                         Started Saying:

Today I Expected: A Naturally Good Feeling Thought:

When I Got Or Did Not Get What I   When I Conversed With Someone
Expected, I: Who Was Feeling Bad About
                                         Themselves Or Complaining, I:

Today I Stretched My Beliefs By: A List Of Some Positive Thoughts I
                                         Had Today That I Did Not Oppose
                                         With Negative Thoughts:

A NEW BELIEF
MORNING THOUGHTS

Date: My Mood:

Today's Affirmation: Today I Am Releasing:

Today's New Beliefs: Today I Am Choosing To Feel:

NIGHTLY THOUGHTS

Today I Chose To See: Today I Noticed A Positive Change In:

Today I Forgave: I Stopped Criticizing Myself And
                                         Started Saying:

Today I Expected: A Naturally Good Feeling Thought:

When I Got Or Did Not Get What I   When I Conversed With Someone
Expected, I: Who Was Feeling Bad About
                                         Themselves Or Complaining, I:

Today I Stretched My Beliefs By: A List Of Some Positive Thoughts I
                                         Had Today That I Did Not Oppose
                                         With Negative Thoughts:

A NEW BELIEF
MORNING THOUGHTS

Date: My Mood:

Today's Affirmation: Today I Am Releasing:

Today's New Beliefs: Today I Am Choosing To Feel:

NIGHTLY THOUGHTS

Today I Chose To See: Today I Noticed A Positive Change In:

Today I Forgave: I Stopped Criticizing Myself And
                                         Started Saying:

Today I Expected: A Naturally Good Feeling Thought:

When I Got Or Did Not Get What I   When I Conversed With Someone
Expected, I: Who Was Feeling Bad About
                                         Themselves Or Complaining, I:

Today I Stretched My Beliefs By: A List Of Some Positive Thoughts I
                                         Had Today That I Did Not Oppose
                                         With Negative Thoughts:

MY POSITIVE THOUGHTS

A NEW BELIEF
MORNING THOUGHTS

Date: My Mood:

Today's Affirmation: Today I Am Releasing:

Today's New Beliefs: Today I Am Choosing To Feel:

NIGHTLY THOUGHTS

Today I Chose To See: Today I Noticed A Positive Change In:

Today I Forgave: I Stopped Criticizing Myself And
                                         Started Saying:

Today I Expected: A Naturally Good Feeling Thought:

When I Got Or Did Not Get What I   When I Conversed With Someone
Expected, I: Who Was Feeling Bad About
                                         Themselves Or Complaining, I:

Today I Stretched My Beliefs By: A List Of Some Positive Thoughts I
                                         Had Today That I Did Not Oppose
                                         With Negative Thoughts:

A NEW BELIEF
MORNING THOUGHTS

Date: My Mood:

Today's Affirmation: Today I Am Releasing:

Today's New Beliefs: Today I Am Choosing To Feel:

NIGHTLY THOUGHTS

Today I Chose To See: Today I Noticed A Positive Change In:

Today I Forgave: I Stopped Criticizing Myself And
                                         Started Saying:

Today I Expected: A Naturally Good Feeling Thought:

When I Got Or Did Not Get What I   When I Conversed With Someone
Expected, I: Who Was Feeling Bad About
                                         Themselves Or Complaining, I:

Today I Stretched My Beliefs By: A List Of Some Positive Thoughts I
                                         Had Today That I Did Not Oppose
                                         With Negative Thoughts:

A NEW BELIEF
MORNING THOUGHTS

Date: My Mood:

Today's Affirmation: Today I Am Releasing:

Today's New Beliefs: Today I Am Choosing To Feel:

NIGHTLY THOUGHTS

Today I Chose To See: Today I Noticed A Positive Change In:

Today I Forgave: I Stopped Criticizing Myself And
                                         Started Saying:

Today I Expected: A Naturally Good Feeling Thought:

When I Got Or Did Not Get What I   When I Conversed With Someone
Expected, I: Who Was Feeling Bad About
                                         Themselves Or Complaining, I:

Today I Stretched My Beliefs By: A List Of Some Positive Thoughts I
                                         Had Today That I Did Not Oppose
                                         With Negative Thoughts:

A NEW BELIEF
MORNING THOUGHTS

Date: My Mood:

Today's Affirmation: Today I Am Releasing:

Today's New Beliefs: Today I Am Choosing To Feel:

NIGHTLY THOUGHTS

Today I Chose To See: Today I Noticed A Positive Change In:

Today I Forgave: I Stopped Criticizing Myself And
                                   Started Saying:

Today I Expected: A Naturally Good Feeling Thought:

When I Got Or Did Not Get What I   When I Conversed With Someone
Expected, I: Who Was Feeling Bad About
                                   Themselves Or Complaining, I:

Today I Stretched My Beliefs By: A List Of Some Positive Thoughts I
                                   Had Today That I Did Not Oppose
                                   With Negative Thoughts:

THERE WILL BE PEOPLE WHO WILL TRY TO BREAK ME AND THOSE WHO WILL EVEN HATE ME AND I WILL STILL CONTINUE TO LIVE A POSITIVE LIFE.

A NEW BELIEF
MORNING THOUGHTS

Date: My Mood:

Today's Affirmation: Today I Am Releasing:

Today's New Beliefs: Today I Am Choosing To Feel:

NIGHTLY THOUGHTS

Today I Chose To See: Today I Noticed A Positive Change In:

Today I Forgave: I Stopped Criticizing Myself And
                                         Started Saying:

Today I Expected: A Naturally Good Feeling Thought:

When I Got Or Did Not Get What I   When I Conversed With Someone
Expected, I: Who Was Feeling Bad About
                                         Themselves Or Complaining, I:

Today I Stretched My Beliefs By: A List Of Some Positive Thoughts I
                                         Had Today That I Did Not Oppose
                                         With Negative Thoughts:

A NEW BELIEF
MORNING THOUGHTS

Date: My Mood:

Today's Affirmation: Today I Am Releasing:

Today's New Beliefs: Today I Am Choosing To Feel:

NIGHTLY THOUGHTS

Today I Chose To See: Today I Noticed A Positive Change In:

Today I Forgave: I Stopped Criticizing Myself And
                                     Started Saying:

Today I Expected: A Naturally Good Feeling Thought:

When I Got Or Did Not Get What I   When I Conversed With Someone
Expected, I: Who Was Feeling Bad About
                                     Themselves Or Complaining, I:

Today I Stretched My Beliefs By: A List Of Some Positive Thoughts I
                                     Had Today That I Did Not Oppose
                                     With Negative Thoughts:

A NEW BELIEF
MORNING THOUGHTS

Date: My Mood:

Today's Affirmation: Today I Am Releasing:

Today's New Beliefs: Today I Am Choosing To Feel:

NIGHTLY THOUGHTS

Today I Chose To See: Today I Noticed A Positive Change In:

Today I Forgave: I Stopped Criticizing Myself And
                                         Started Saying:

Today I Expected: A Naturally Good Feeling Thought:

When I Got Or Did Not Get What I   When I Conversed With Someone
Expected, I: Who Was Feeling Bad About
                                         Themselves Or Complaining, I:

Today I Stretched My Beliefs By: A List Of Some Positive Thoughts I
                                         Had Today That I Did Not Oppose
                                         With Negative Thoughts:

I WILL BE AN ENCOURAGER TO MYSELF AND OTHERS.

A NEW BELIEF
MORNING THOUGHTS

Date: My Mood:

Today's Affirmation: Today I Am Releasing:

Today's New Beliefs: Today I Am Choosing To Feel:

NIGHTLY THOUGHTS

Today I Chose To See: Today I Noticed A Positive Change In:

Today I Forgave: I Stopped Criticizing Myself And
                                     Started Saying:

Today I Expected: A Naturally Good Feeling Thought:

When I Got Or Did Not Get What I   When I Conversed With Someone
Expected, I: Who Was Feeling Bad About
                                     Themselves Or Complaining, I:

Today I Stretched My Beliefs By: A List Of Some Positive Thoughts I
                                     Had Today That I Did Not Oppose
                                     With Negative Thoughts:

A NEW BELIEF
MORNING THOUGHTS

Date: My Mood:

Today's Affirmation: Today I Am Releasing:

Today's New Beliefs: Today I Am Choosing To Feel:

NIGHTLY THOUGHTS

Today I Chose To See: Today I Noticed A Positive Change In:

Today I Forgave: I Stopped Criticizing Myself And
                                               Started Saying:

Today I Expected: A Naturally Good Feeling Thought:

When I Got Or Did Not Get What I   When I Conversed With Someone
Expected, I: Who Was Feeling Bad About
                                               Themselves Or Complaining, I:

Today I Stretched My Beliefs By: A List Of Some Positive Thoughts I
                                               Had Today That I Did Not Oppose
                                               With Negative Thoughts:

A NEW BELIEF
MORNING THOUGHTS

Date: My Mood:

Today's Affirmation: Today I Am Releasing:

Today's New Beliefs: Today I Am Choosing To Feel:

NIGHTLY THOUGHTS

Today I Chose To See: Today I Noticed A Positive Change In:

Today I Forgave: I Stopped Criticizing Myself And
                                         Started Saying:

Today I Expected: A Naturally Good Feeling Thought:

When I Got Or Did Not Get What I   When I Conversed With Someone
Expected, I: Who Was Feeling Bad About
                                         Themselves Or Complaining, I:

Today I Stretched My Beliefs By: A List Of Some Positive Thoughts I
                                         Had Today That I Did Not Oppose
                                         With Negative Thoughts:

A NEW BELIEF
MORNING THOUGHTS

Date: My Mood:

Today's Affirmation: Today I Am Releasing:

Today's New Beliefs: Today I Am Choosing To Feel:

NIGHTLY THOUGHTS

Today I Chose To See: Today I Noticed A Positive Change In:

Today I Forgave: I Stopped Criticizing Myself And
                               Started Saying:

Today I Expected: A Naturally Good Feeling Thought:

When I Got Or Did Not Get What I   When I Conversed With Someone
Expected, I: Who Was Feeling Bad About
                                    Themselves Or Complaining, I:

Today I Stretched My Beliefs By: A List Of Some Positive Thoughts I
                                    Had Today That I Did Not Oppose
                                    With Negative Thoughts:

A NEW BELIEF
MORNING THOUGHTS

Date: My Mood:

Today's Affirmation: Today I Am Releasing:

Today's New Beliefs: Today I Am Choosing To Feel:

NIGHTLY THOUGHTS

Today I Chose To See: Today I Noticed A Positive Change In:

Today I Forgave: I Stopped Criticizing Myself And
                                         Started Saying:

Today I Expected: A Naturally Good Feeling Thought:

When I Got Or Did Not Get What I   When I Conversed With Someone
Expected, I: Who Was Feeling Bad About
                                         Themselves Or Complaining, I:

Today I Stretched My Beliefs By: A List Of Some Positive Thoughts I
                                         Had Today That I Did Not Oppose
                                         With Negative Thoughts:

I REJECT EVERY NEGATIVE THOUGHT.

I CHOOSE TO BE OPEN. I CHOOSE TO BE VULNERABLE. I CHOOSE TO TAKE RISKS. NO LONGER WILL I LIVE WITH THOUGHTS THAT WILL NOT ALLOW ME TO BE MY BEST.

A NEW BELIEF
MORNING THOUGHTS

Date: My Mood:

Today's Affirmation: Today I Am Releasing:

Today's New Beliefs: Today I Am Choosing To Feel:

NIGHTLY THOUGHTS

Today I Chose To See: Today I Noticed A Positive Change In:

Today I Forgave: I Stopped Criticizing Myself And
                               Started Saying:

Today I Expected: A Naturally Good Feeling Thought:

When I Got Or Did Not Get What I   When I Conversed With Someone
Expected, I: Who Was Feeling Bad About
                                   Themselves Or Complaining, I:

Today I Stretched My Beliefs By: A List Of Some Positive Thoughts I
                                   Had Today That I Did Not Oppose
                                   With Negative Thoughts:

A NEW BELIEF
MORNING THOUGHTS

Date: My Mood:

Today's Affirmation: Today I Am Releasing:

Today's New Beliefs: Today I Am Choosing To Feel:

NIGHTLY THOUGHTS

Today I Chose To See: Today I Noticed A Positive Change In:

Today I Forgave: I Stopped Criticizing Myself And
                                         Started Saying:

Today I Expected: A Naturally Good Feeling Thought:

When I Got Or Did Not Get What I   When I Conversed With Someone
Expected, I: Who Was Feeling Bad About
                                         Themselves Or Complaining, I:

Today I Stretched My Beliefs By: A List Of Some Positive Thoughts I
                                         Had Today That I Did Not Oppose
                                         With Negative Thoughts:

A NEW BELIEF
MORNING THOUGHTS

Date: My Mood:

Today's Affirmation: Today I Am Releasing:

Today's New Beliefs: Today I Am Choosing To Feel:

NIGHTLY THOUGHTS

Today I Chose To See: Today I Noticed A Positive Change In:

Today I Forgave: I Stopped Criticizing Myself And
                                     Started Saying:

Today I Expected: A Naturally Good Feeling Thought:

When I Got Or Did Not Get What I   When I Conversed With Someone
Expected, I: Who Was Feeling Bad About
                                     Themselves Or Complaining, I:

Today I Stretched My Beliefs By: A List Of Some Positive Thoughts I
                                     Had Today That I Did Not Oppose
                                     With Negative Thoughts:

I LOVE IT WHEN MY MIND TELLS ME ABOUT MY GREATNESS.

MY POSITIVE THOUGHTS

A NEW BELIEF
MORNING THOUGHTS

Date: My Mood:

Today's Affirmation: Today I Am Releasing:

Today's New Beliefs: Today I Am Choosing To Feel:

NIGHTLY THOUGHTS

Today I Chose To See: Today I Noticed A Positive Change In:

Today I Forgave: I Stopped Criticizing Myself And
                                   Started Saying:

Today I Expected: A Naturally Good Feeling Thought:

When I Got Or Did Not Get What I   When I Conversed With Someone
Expected, I: Who Was Feeling Bad About
                                   Themselves Or Complaining, I:

Today I Stretched My Beliefs By: A List Of Some Positive Thoughts I
                                   Had Today That I Did Not Oppose
                                   With Negative Thoughts:

A NEW BELIEF
MORNING THOUGHTS

Date: My Mood:

Today's Affirmation: Today I Am Releasing:

Today's New Beliefs: Today I Am Choosing To Feel:

NIGHTLY THOUGHTS

Today I Chose To See: Today I Noticed A Positive Change In:

Today I Forgave: I Stopped Criticizing Myself And
                                Started Saying:

Today I Expected: A Naturally Good Feeling Thought:

When I Got Or Did Not Get What I   When I Conversed With Someone
Expected, I: Who Was Feeling Bad About
                                    Themselves Or Complaining, I:

Today I Stretched My Beliefs By: A List Of Some Positive Thoughts I
                                    Had Today That I Did Not Oppose
                                    With Negative Thoughts:

A NEW BELIEF
MORNING THOUGHTS

Date: My Mood:

Today's Affirmation: Today I Am Releasing:

Today's New Beliefs: Today I Am Choosing To Feel:

NIGHTLY THOUGHTS

Today I Chose To See: Today I Noticed A Positive Change In:

Today I Forgave: I Stopped Criticizing Myself And Started Saying:

Today I Expected: A Naturally Good Feeling Thought:

When I Got Or Did Not Get What I Expected, I: When I Conversed With Someone Who Was Feeling Bad About Themselves Or Complaining, I:

Today I Stretched My Beliefs By: A List Of Some Positive Thoughts I Had Today That I Did Not Oppose With Negative Thoughts:

I CHOOSE TO FOCUS ON WHAT I HAVE, NOT WHAT I LACK.

WHAT CONSUMES MY MIND IS LOVE.

A NEW BELIEF
MORNING THOUGHTS

Date: My Mood:

Today's Affirmation: Today I Am Releasing:

Today's New Beliefs: Today I Am Choosing To Feel:

NIGHTLY THOUGHTS

Today I Chose To See: Today I Noticed A Positive Change In:

Today I Forgave: I Stopped Criticizing Myself And
                                         Started Saying:

Today I Expected: A Naturally Good Feeling Thought:

When I Got Or Did Not Get What I   When I Conversed With Someone
Expected, I: Who Was Feeling Bad About
                                         Themselves Or Complaining, I:

Today I Stretched My Beliefs By: A List Of Some Positive Thoughts I
                                         Had Today That I Did Not Oppose
                                         With Negative Thoughts:

A NEW BELIEF
MORNING THOUGHTS

Date: My Mood:

Today's Affirmation: Today I Am Releasing:

Today's New Beliefs: Today I Am Choosing To Feel:

NIGHTLY THOUGHTS

Today I Chose To See: Today I Noticed A Positive Change In:

Today I Forgave: I Stopped Criticizing Myself And
                                         Started Saying:

Today I Expected: A Naturally Good Feeling Thought:

When I Got Or Did Not Get What I   When I Conversed With Someone
Expected, I: Who Was Feeling Bad About
                                         Themselves Or Complaining, I:

Today I Stretched My Beliefs By: A List Of Some Positive Thoughts I
                                         Had Today That I Did Not Oppose
                                         With Negative Thoughts:

MY POSITIVE THOUGHTS

A NEW BELIEF
MORNING THOUGHTS

Date: My Mood:

Today's Affirmation: Today I Am Releasing:

Today's New Beliefs: Today I Am Choosing To Feel:

NIGHTLY THOUGHTS

Today I Chose To See: Today I Noticed A Positive Change In:

Today I Forgave: I Stopped Criticizing Myself And
                                     Started Saying:

Today I Expected: A Naturally Good Feeling Thought:

When I Got Or Did Not Get What I   When I Conversed With Someone
Expected, I: Who Was Feeling Bad About
                                     Themselves Or Complaining, I:

Today I Stretched My Beliefs By: A List Of Some Positive Thoughts I
                                     Had Today That I Did Not Oppose
                                     With Negative Thoughts:

A NEW BELIEF
MORNING THOUGHTS

Date: My Mood:

Today's Affirmation: Today I Am Releasing:

Today's New Beliefs: Today I Am Choosing To Feel:

NIGHTLY THOUGHTS

Today I Chose To See: Today I Noticed A Positive Change In:

Today I Forgave: I Stopped Criticizing Myself And
                                         Started Saying:

Today I Expected: A Naturally Good Feeling Thought:

When I Got Or Did Not Get What I   When I Conversed With Someone
Expected, I: Who Was Feeling Bad About
                                         Themselves Or Complaining, I:

Today I Stretched My Beliefs By: A List Of Some Positive Thoughts I
                                         Had Today That I Did Not Oppose
                                         With Negative Thoughts:

A NEW BELIEF
MORNING THOUGHTS

Date: My Mood:

Today's Affirmation: Today I Am Releasing:

Today's New Beliefs: Today I Am Choosing To Feel:

NIGHTLY THOUGHTS

Today I Chose To See: Today I Noticed A Positive Change In:

Today I Forgave: I Stopped Criticizing Myself And
                                         Started Saying:

Today I Expected: A Naturally Good Feeling Thought:

When I Got Or Did Not Get What I   When I Conversed With Someone
Expected, I: Who Was Feeling Bad About
                                         Themselves Or Complaining, I:

Today I Stretched My Beliefs By: A List Of Some Positive Thoughts I
                                         Had Today That I Did Not Oppose
                                         With Negative Thoughts:

IT IS OKAY TO HAVE NEGATIVE THOUGHTS, IT IS NOT OKAY TO DWELL IN THEM. IF THEY COME LET THEM GO. GIVE THEM NO ATTENTION.

EVEN WHEN MY MIND TRIES TO DISCOURAGE ME, GOD'S WORD LIFTS ME RIGHT UP.

A NEW BELIEF
MORNING THOUGHTS

Date: My Mood:

Today's Affirmation: Today I Am Releasing:

Today's New Beliefs: Today I Am Choosing To Feel:

NIGHTLY THOUGHTS

Today I Chose To See: Today I Noticed A Positive Change In:

Today I Forgave: I Stopped Criticizing Myself And
                                         Started Saying:

Today I Expected: A Naturally Good Feeling Thought:

When I Got Or Did Not Get What I   When I Conversed With Someone
Expected, I: Who Was Feeling Bad About
                                         Themselves Or Complaining, I:

Today I Stretched My Beliefs By: A List Of Some Positive Thoughts I
                                         Had Today That I Did Not Oppose
                                         With Negative Thoughts:

A NEW BELIEF
MORNING THOUGHTS

Date: My Mood:

Today's Affirmation: Today I Am Releasing:

Today's New Beliefs: Today I Am Choosing To Feel:

NIGHTLY THOUGHTS

Today I Chose To See: Today I Noticed A Positive Change In:

Today I Forgave: I Stopped Criticizing Myself And
                               Started Saying:

Today I Expected: A Naturally Good Feeling Thought:

When I Got Or Did Not Get What I   When I Conversed With Someone
Expected, I: Who Was Feeling Bad About
                                    Themselves Or Complaining, I:

Today I Stretched My Beliefs By: A List Of Some Positive Thoughts I
                                    Had Today That I Did Not Oppose
                                    With Negative Thoughts:

A NEW BELIEF
MORNING THOUGHTS

Date: My Mood:

Today's Affirmation: Today I Am Releasing:

Today's New Beliefs: Today I Am Choosing To Feel:

NIGHTLY THOUGHTS

Today I Chose To See: Today I Noticed A Positive Change In:

Today I Forgave: I Stopped Criticizing Myself And
                                   Started Saying:

Today I Expected: A Naturally Good Feeling Thought:

When I Got Or Did Not Get What I   When I Conversed With Someone
Expected, I: Who Was Feeling Bad About
                                   Themselves Or Complaining, I:

Today I Stretched My Beliefs By: A List Of Some Positive Thoughts I
                                   Had Today That I Did Not Oppose
                                   With Negative Thoughts:

MY MINDSET IS CHANGING. I AM ONLY GETTING WISER.

NO LONGER WILL I ALLOW BAD THOUGHTS TO LIVE IN MY HEAD.

A NEW BELIEF
MORNING THOUGHTS

Date: My Mood:

Today's Affirmation: Today I Am Releasing:

Today's New Beliefs: Today I Am Choosing To Feel:

NIGHTLY THOUGHTS

Today I Chose To See: Today I Noticed A Positive Change In:

Today I Forgave: I Stopped Criticizing Myself And
                                           Started Saying:

Today I Expected: A Naturally Good Feeling Thought:

When I Got Or Did Not Get What I   When I Conversed With Someone
Expected, I: Who Was Feeling Bad About
                                           Themselves Or Complaining, I:

Today I Stretched My Beliefs By: A List Of Some Positive Thoughts I
                                           Had Today That I Did Not Oppose
                                           With Negative Thoughts:

A NEW BELIEF
MORNING THOUGHTS

Date: My Mood:

Today's Affirmation: Today I Am Releasing:

Today's New Beliefs: Today I Am Choosing To Feel:

NIGHTLY THOUGHTS

Today I Chose To See: Today I Noticed A Positive Change In:

Today I Forgave: I Stopped Criticizing Myself And
                                         Started Saying:

Today I Expected: A Naturally Good Feeling Thought:

When I Got Or Did Not Get What I   When I Conversed With Someone
Expected, I: Who Was Feeling Bad About
                                         Themselves Or Complaining, I:

Today I Stretched My Beliefs By: A List Of Some Positive Thoughts I
                                         Had Today That I Did Not Oppose
                                         With Negative Thoughts:

A NEW BELIEF
MORNING THOUGHTS

Date: My Mood:

Today's Affirmation: Today I Am Releasing:

Today's New Beliefs: Today I Am Choosing To Feel:

NIGHTLY THOUGHTS

Today I Chose To See: Today I Noticed A Positive Change In:

Today I Forgave: I Stopped Criticizing Myself And
                                   Started Saying:

Today I Expected: A Naturally Good Feeling Thought:

When I Got Or Did Not Get What I   When I Conversed With Someone
Expected, I: Who Was Feeling Bad About
                                   Themselves Or Complaining, I:

Today I Stretched My Beliefs By: A List Of Some Positive Thoughts I
                                   Had Today That I Did Not Oppose
                                   With Negative Thoughts:

MY POSITIVE THOUGHTS

A NEW BELIEF
MORNING THOUGHTS

Date: My Mood:

Today's Affirmation: Today I Am Releasing:

Today's New Beliefs: Today I Am Choosing To Feel:

NIGHTLY THOUGHTS

Today I Chose To See: Today I Noticed A Positive Change In:

Today I Forgave: I Stopped Criticizing Myself And
                                     Started Saying:

Today I Expected: A Naturally Good Feeling Thought:

When I Got Or Did Not Get What I   When I Conversed With Someone
Expected, I: Who Was Feeling Bad About
                                     Themselves Or Complaining, I:

Today I Stretched My Beliefs By: A List Of Some Positive Thoughts I
                                     Had Today That I Did Not Oppose
                                     With Negative Thoughts:

A NEW BELIEF
MORNING THOUGHTS

Date: My Mood:

Today's Affirmation: Today I Am Releasing:

Today's New Beliefs: Today I Am Choosing To Feel:

NIGHTLY THOUGHTS

Today I Chose To See: Today I Noticed A Positive Change In:

Today I Forgave: I Stopped Criticizing Myself And
                                         Started Saying:

Today I Expected: A Naturally Good Feeling Thought:

When I Got Or Did Not Get What I   When I Conversed With Someone
Expected, I: Who Was Feeling Bad About
                                         Themselves Or Complaining, I:

Today I Stretched My Beliefs By: A List Of Some Positive Thoughts I
                                         Had Today That I Did Not Oppose
                                         With Negative Thoughts:

EVERYTHING WILL BE OKAY.

A NEW BELIEF
MORNING THOUGHTS

Date: My Mood:

Today's Affirmation: Today I Am Releasing:

Today's New Beliefs: Today I Am Choosing To Feel:

NIGHTLY THOUGHTS

Today I Chose To See: Today I Noticed A Positive Change In:

Today I Forgave: I Stopped Criticizing Myself And
                                   Started Saying:

Today I Expected: A Naturally Good Feeling Thought:

When I Got Or Did Not Get What I   When I Conversed With Someone
Expected, I: Who Was Feeling Bad About
                                   Themselves Or Complaining, I:

Today I Stretched My Beliefs By: A List Of Some Positive Thoughts I
                                   Had Today That I Did Not Oppose
                                   With Negative Thoughts:

A NEW BELIEF
MORNING THOUGHTS

Date: My Mood:

Today's Affirmation: Today I Am Releasing:

Today's New Beliefs: Today I Am Choosing To Feel:

NIGHTLY THOUGHTS

Today I Chose To See: Today I Noticed A Positive Change In:

Today I Forgave: I Stopped Criticizing Myself And
                                Started Saying:

Today I Expected: A Naturally Good Feeling Thought:

When I Got Or Did Not Get What I   When I Conversed With Someone
Expected, I: Who Was Feeling Bad About
                                Themselves Or Complaining, I:

Today I Stretched My Beliefs By: A List Of Some Positive Thoughts I
                                Had Today That I Did Not Oppose
                                With Negative Thoughts:

A NEW BELIEF
MORNING THOUGHTS

Date: My Mood:

Today's Affirmation: Today I Am Releasing:

Today's New Beliefs: Today I Am Choosing To Feel:

NIGHTLY THOUGHTS

Today I Chose To See: Today I Noticed A Positive Change In:

Today I Forgave: I Stopped Criticizing Myself And
                                   Started Saying:

Today I Expected: A Naturally Good Feeling Thought:

When I Got Or Did Not Get What I   When I Conversed With Someone
Expected, I: Who Was Feeling Bad About
                                   Themselves Or Complaining, I:

Today I Stretched My Beliefs By: A List Of Some Positive Thoughts I
                                   Had Today That I Did Not Oppose
                                   With Negative Thoughts:

I AM NO LONGER A PRISONER TO NEGATIVE THOUGHTS.

A NEW BELIEF
MORNING THOUGHTS

Date: My Mood:

Today's Affirmation: Today I Am Releasing:

Today's New Beliefs: Today I Am Choosing To Feel:

NIGHTLY THOUGHTS

Today I Chose To See: Today I Noticed A Positive Change In:

Today I Forgave: I Stopped Criticizing Myself And
                                        Started Saying:

Today I Expected: A Naturally Good Feeling Thought:

When I Got Or Did Not Get What I   When I Conversed With Someone
Expected, I: Who Was Feeling Bad About
                                        Themselves Or Complaining, I:

Today I Stretched My Beliefs By: A List Of Some Positive Thoughts I
                                        Had Today That I Did Not Oppose
                                        With Negative Thoughts:

A NEW BELIEF
MORNING THOUGHTS

Date: My Mood:

Today's Affirmation: Today I Am Releasing:

Today's New Beliefs: Today I Am Choosing To Feel:

NIGHTLY THOUGHTS

Today I Chose To See: Today I Noticed A Positive Change In:

Today I Forgave: I Stopped Criticizing Myself And
                                         Started Saying:

Today I Expected: A Naturally Good Feeling Thought:

When I Got Or Did Not Get What I   When I Conversed With Someone
Expected, I: Who Was Feeling Bad About
                                         Themselves Or Complaining, I:

Today I Stretched My Beliefs By: A List Of Some Positive Thoughts I
                                         Had Today That I Did Not Oppose
                                         With Negative Thoughts:

NO LONGER AM I AFRAID TO TRY.

A NEW BELIEF
MORNING THOUGHTS

Date:

My Mood:

Today's Affirmation:

Today I Am Releasing:

Today's New Beliefs:

Today I Am Choosing To Feel:

NIGHTLY THOUGHTS

Today I Chose To See:

Today I Noticed A Positive Change In:

Today I Forgave:

I Stopped Criticizing Myself And Started Saying:

Today I Expected:

A Naturally Good Feeling Thought:

When I Got Or Did Not Get What I Expected, I:

When I Conversed With Someone Who Was Feeling Bad About Themselves Or Complaining, I:

Today I Stretched My Beliefs By:

A List Of Some Positive Thoughts I Had Today That I Did Not Oppose With Negative Thoughts:

I AM THE FRUIT OF MY THOUGHTS.